	DATE DUE		

My gran
dres
Author:
Reading Level: 1.2 LG
Point Value: 0.5
ACCELERATED READER QUIZ# 54470

W9-ANM-404

162059

646.4
HUG
C.1

Hughes, Sarah.

**My grandmother works
in a dress shop**

DISCARD

ALICE GUSTAFSON ELEMENTARY LRC

325064 00886   55763D   001

046.4
tuG
c.1

My Family at Work

My Grandmother Works in a Dress Shop

By Sarah Hughes

ALICE GUSTAFSON
SCHOOL
LEARNING CENTER

Children's Press
A Division of Scholastic Inc.
New York / Toronto / London / Auckland / Sydney
Mexico City / New Delhi / Hong Kong
Danbury, Connecticut

Thanks to Barbara Harris Custom Design in Philadelphia and Mary Harris

Photo Credits: Cover and all photos by Maura Boruchow
Contributing Editors: Jeri Cipriano, Jennifer Silate
Book Design: Michael DeLisio

Visit Children's Press on the Internet at:
http://publishing.grolier.com

Library of Congress Cataloging-in-Publication Data

Hughes, Sarah, 1964—
    My grandmother works in a dress shop / by Sarah Hughes.
    p. cm.— (My family at work)
    Includes index.
    ISBN 0-516-23180-4 (lib. bdg.) — ISBN 0-516-29576-4 (pbk.)
    1. Dressmaking—Juvenile literature. 2. Dressmakers—Juvenile literature. [1.
        Dressmaking. 2. Occupations.] I. Title.

TT515 .H84 2000
646.4'0092—dc21

00-047535

Copyright © 2001 by Rosen Book Works, Inc.
All rights reserved. Published simultaneously in Canada.
Printed in the United States of America.
    4 5 6 7 8 9 10 R 05 04

Contents

My name is Keisha.

This is my **grandmother**.

Grandma works in a dress shop.

Today she will make a dress for me.

Grandma helps me choose a **fabric**.

I choose red fabric.

Now Grandma **measures** me.

10

Grandma pins the fabric to the paper dress **pattern**.

I help her.

13

Grandma cuts the fabric for my dress.

15

Grandma **sews** my dress.

ALICE GUSTAFSON
SCHOOL
LEARNING CENTER

16

Grandma makes sure my dress fits.

All done!

How do you like my new dress?

New Words

fabric (**fab**-rihk) cloth

grandmother (**grand**-muhth-uhr) the mother
   of your mother or father

measures (**mehzh**-uhrz) finds the size
   of something

pattern (**pat**-uhrn) a guide for something
   you make

sews (**sohz**) pushes a needle and thread
   through cloth

To Find Out More

Books
Bruno the Tailor
by Lars Klinting
Henry Holt & Company

The Purple Coat
by Amy Hest
Aladdin Paperbacks

Web Site
Sew Young, Sew Fun!
http://www.sewyoungsewfun.com
This Web site has information about sewing, project ideas,
and contests that can be completed with the help of an adult.

Index

About the Author
Sarah Hughes is from New York City and taught school for twelve years. She is now writing and editing children's books. In her free time she enjoys running and riding her bike.

Reading Consultants

Kris Flynn, Coordinator, Small School District Literacy, The San Diego County Office of Education

Shelly Forys, Certified Reading Recovery Specialist, W.J. Zahnow Elementary School, Waterloo, IL

Sue McAdams, Certified Reading Recovery Specialist and Literary Consultant, Dallas, TX

ALICE GUSTAFSON
SCHOOL
LEARNING CENTER